Erni Cabat's magical world
of dinosaurs

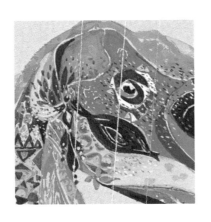

ERNI CABAT'S
MAGICAL WORLD OF

DINOSAURS

PAINTINGS BY
ERNI CABAT

ERNI CABAT'S
MAGICAL
WORLD OF

DINOSAURS

POETRY BY
LOLLIE BUTLER

GREAT · IMPRESSIONS

TUCSON
ARIZONA

ACKNOWLEDGEMENT

Science travels in small steps. What we know about dinosaurs has come in actual bits and real pieces; it has been the work of generations of paleontologists, zooarchaeologists, model makers, curators and many others to put things back together again. And the work is not finished yet; the nature of science is that it never will be. Erni Cabat would like to thank all the people whose work inspired his own vision of these dazzling creatures. The dinosaurs left them little enough to go by, and it all happened so long ago.

Art copyright © 1989 by Erni Cabat.
Poetry copyright © 1989 by Lollie Butler.

Published by:
GREAT IMPRESSIONS
an imprint of Great Arts Press, Inc.
55 West Adams, Suite 210
P.O. Box 65270
Tucson, Arizona 85740-2270
(602) 882-5100

ISBN 0-925263-01-X
Library of Congress Catalog Number: 89-80188

Designed by Erni Cabat.
Edited by Michael Rule.
Color separations by American Color Corporation.
Lithography by Fabe Litho, Ltd.
Binding by Roswell Bookbinding.

Printed in U.S.A.
10 9 8 7 6 5 4 3 2

Library of Congress Cataloging-in-Publication Data

Cabat, Erni.
    Erni Cabat's magical world of dinosaurs.

    Summary: Presents paintings of several dinosaurs accompanied by humorous poems.
    1. Cabat, Erni—Juvenile literature.   2. Dinosaurs in art—Juvenile literature.   [1. Dinosaurs in art. 2. Dinosaurs—Poetry]   I. Butler, Lollie, 1938- II. Title: Magical world of dinosaurs.   III. Title: Dinosaurs.
ND237.C14A4   1989   759.13   89-80188
ISBN 0-925263-01-X

TABLE OF CONTENTS

DEDICATION

To people everywhere who have the courage to dream,
who set free their imaginations and dare to live
in the world of why . . . what if . . . and why not!
It's a wonderland, open only to children of all ages.

FOREWORD

Over the past forty years I have seen and referred to many of the well-illustrated texts for young people that deal with fossil animals. When I was very young these volumes inspired me to make the study of fossil vertebrates my life's work. These earlier works all had one thing in common—the fossil animals, particularly reptiles, had the restoration colored like the scale patterns of living reptiles and lacked life.

When I first saw Erni Cabat's illustrations, I was impressed by his vivid use of colors and patterns without distorting the features or proportions of the animals depicted. They are reminiscent of the beautiful artwork of the Australian aboriginies who portray their kangaroos and crocodiles in bright zigzags of white and brown yet you are quite aware of the exact animal the artist had in mind. I have also seen the dyed batiks in the markets of Nepal and Tibet that have similar portrayals of elephants, sacred cattle, and yaks all in rainbow colors. It is refreshing to see a triceratops that doesn't look like an expanded version of a horned lizard in dull brown or grey tones.

Stanley J. Olsen

Stanley J. Olsen is the curator of zooarchaeology at the Arizona State Museum and a professor of anthropology at the University of Arizona. The author of nearly 200 scientific articles, books and other publications, professor Olsen has been working with bones since 1945.

JUST

SUPPOSE...

Do you suppose that dinosaurs
came in shades of pink,
or yellow, blue and orange too?
Now tell me what you think.

In tracking down the dinosaur
some scientists, I'm told,
cannot agree on whether he
was warm or was he cold?

According to the tracks we've found
they ran through mud and clay.
Do you suppose if they'd slowed down
they'd be alive today?

To breakfast with a dinosaur
would be a treat, you bet.
And ride a dinosaur to school,
or keep one for a pet.

Perhaps Tyrannosaurus Rex
had very ticklish toes.
We don't know all about them but
it's fun to just suppose!

A Halloween Trick

I love Halloween! It's my favorite day,
but accidents happen. It happened this way:
I said to my mother one day about three,
"I'll go trick-or-treating, but what can I be?"

"I want to be something that no one will guess.
My Halloween costume must be just the best."
Mother stopped thinking and smiled as she said,
"Be a Triceratops, with horns on your head!"

"We'll make a neat costume of velvet and tin."
So she sewed up the costume and zippered me in.
I tricked and I treated and had lots of fun,
but the zipper is stuck and it won't come undone!

Now Halloween's past and I look like a fool.
I wear it to play and I wear it to school.
The kids laugh and joke and they tease me a lot;
I can't eat my lunch and it's sure getting hot!

I've had some bad luck with the costume we picked;
I wanted a treat, but instead I got tricked!
I'm here in this costume, as mad as can be,
Halloween's over and I want to be ME!

Triceratops
try-SER-uh-tops

A Lucky Fellow

Dimetrodon's very lucky
with his built-in sail;
while lying in the winter sun
it warms him head to tail.

It cools him in the summer shade.
(No sweat upon his face!)
It's really quite a handy thing
to carry place to place.

Dimetrodon
dye-MET-tro-don

Hesperonis, The Watercolored Duck

This rare bird is happy
his coat is so snappy,
he's not a dull bird any more.

His suit was once duller,
but he used watercolor,
to paint a design they'd adore.

But since he's a swimmer,
his coat will grow dimmer,
when he swims to parties ashore.

But no one will snub him,
his friends will still love him,
when his coat's as plain as before.

Hesperornis
hes-per-OR-nis

Rusty's Favorite Toy

Lambeosaurus was once just a toy,
the favorite plaything of one little boy.
Rusty would give him a kiss on the head
each night when his mother tucked them into bed.

The story of how Lambie grew with such speed
is one of the funniest stories indeed.
You can see how he looked before he grew tall,
there, in the corner. See, wasn't he small?

But Rusty had habits that weren't very good;
he wouldn't eat spinach, or other green food.
He gave them to Lambeosaurus instead,
until the poor creature grew out of the bed!

Too big for checkers and too big for cards,
too big for houses and too big for yards.
So Rusty's poor dad had to cut a great hole
in the top of their roof (it got pretty cold!)
where Lambeosaurus could stand and look out.
When people would see him, they'd faint or they'd shout.

But all Rusty's friends, the girls and the boys,
loved to come over and play with his toys.
Loved to use Lambie's tail for a slide,
and if they were good, they could go for a ride.

The moral of this story comes at the finish:
Be careful with veggies, especially spinach!

Pachy's and Scrachy's Party

This is the story (now don't you dare try it)
of a birthday party that turned to a riot.
Pachy and Scrachy had strangely striped skins
and long funny toenails: These brothers were twins.

On their four-hundredth birthday their mother said, "Boys,
please clean up your room and pick up your toys.
Your friends are arriving with presents for you;
I'm going for ice cream. Be back in a few!"

No sooner had Mother gone clear out of sight
than these birthday boys picked a horrible fight.
They couldn't decide who would open the gifts,
and Pachy said, "Me first." It started the tiff.
When Scrachy called Pachy some terrible names,
the others stopped playing the new birthday games.

The two hit and punched and butted their heads,
then Mother came back and sent them to bed.
With bumps on their noggins, a terrible ache,
and no mushroom ice cream,
and no cockroach cake.

Pachycephalosaurus
PAK-ee-CEF-al-oh-SAW-rus

Oviraptors, The Egg Bandits

These four-legged creatures are handsome, it's true,
but be on the lookout, for these bandits do
love to steal all of your eggs from you!

They haven't a tooth in their colorful heads,
no uppers or lowers in glasses by beds.
They can't chew on celery, they never eat steak,
no crunchy brown french fries, or chocolate cake.

Just eggs boiled or bubbled, eggs for the pickin'.
They even like eggs that come right from the chicken!
Eggs in an omelet that fries in the pan,
eggs that are squishy and warm in your hand.

Eggs that are scrambled and you ask for more,
eggs that go PLOP-O when dropped on the floor.

These boys are so quiet, they don't make a peep;
they sneak in your kitchen when you are asleep.
Then into your closet they hide with your shoes,
licking and munching the eggs that they choose.

So be on the caution for any strange noise—
it may be the likes of these egg-stealing boys.

Oviraptor
o-vee-RAP-tor

Chasmo's Musical Career

Last Friday the symphony went to the zoo,
but the animals wanted to play music too.
So they handed out flutes and trumpets that tooted;
the monkeys played drums and the elephants hooted.

The animals loved it, their very own band;
the audience laughed and gave them a hand.
But one funny fellow, old Chasmo B. Saurus,
had no instrument to play in the chorus.

"I can't play the tuba," he said with a tear,
"the bagpipes or banjo. I've got a tin ear!"
Which, come to think of it probably meant
he couldn't play music on one instrument.

So they hooked up a music box, shiny and new,
on top of his back, so he plays music too!
Now, when you wind up his tail (it's so long)
he plays "Pop Goes the Weasel," a wonderful song.

Chasmosaurus
KAZ-muh-SAW-rus

15

Too-Big Brachio

Meet Brachiosaurus, a miserable lady.
She sits in a pond where it's cool and it's shady,
chewing on lichens and tops of a beet,
and other weird things that we wouldn't eat!

Brachio chews and she sits like a lump,
trying to lose fifty tons from her rump.
She's big, but believe me, she used to be bigger;
she ate San Francisco and lost her slim figure.

She didn't look good in her pretty prom dress,
so she went on a diet of green watercress,
the roots of petunias and crab dangle greens,
and on Saturday night eats a few pinto beans.

She diets like crazy, she never eats meats,
or chocolate chip cookies or other such treats.
Now her neck and her face are as thin as can be,
but the rest of her body's as big as a tree.

So she chews and she chews and she might think it fair,
to come over to your house and chew on your hair!

Brachiosaurus
BRACK-ee-oh-SAW-rus

The Visitor

I'm Fred Stegosaurus, remember me?
Though I'm very handsome, I'm hard to see.
It's awfully silly, when you come to think,
that I'm so outdated, in fact I'm extinct!

Like lollipops growing on top of a tree,
which means, I suppose, there's no more of me.
But you can discover my face in a book,
or under your bed with the dust, if you look.

I've come back to visit, I really can't stay.
If zookeepers catch me, they'll put me away.
So be kind to animals older than you,
and some day your children will smile at us too.

Like leopards, gorillas and mighty big whales,
pandas and rhinos with very short tails.
I've come a long way and I'm dead on my feet,
so if you don't mind, give me something to eat!

Stegosaurus
STEG-uh-saw-rus

The Archaeopteryx Cannot Fly

So many million years ago
this creature had a choice:
Should he become a reptile,
or keep his bird-like voice?

He chose to keep his feathers,
but I cannot tell you why.
His wings are really lazy,
and do not help him fly.

He's obviously angry now,
he's putting up a howl.
(I've heard he's great-grandfather
to the eagle and the owl.)

He'd like to visit relatives
he's never even met,
but if this bird gets off the ground,
he'll have to use a jet!

Archaeopteryx
are-key-OP-ter-ix

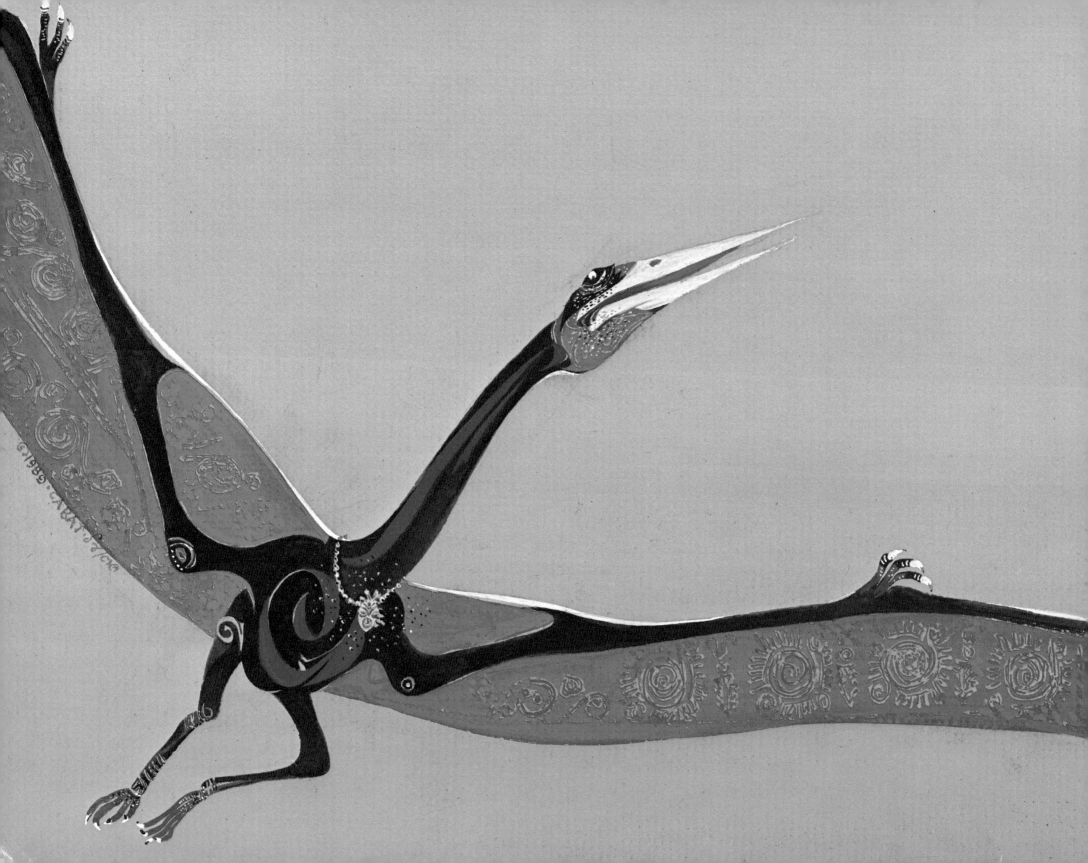

The Emperor's Messenger

A message from the emperor,
a message locked inside.
(Say, isn't this the strangest creature
you have ever spied?)

The emperor was without a wife,
and so he did decide
to find the truest in the land
and she would be his bride.
She'll sit upon the diamond throne,
with golden dogs to mind her.
The swiftest messenger he sent,
in hopes that he would find her.

He didn't have an envelope,
he didn't have a pocket,
so they wrote the message in Chinese
and sealed it in a locket.
A message from the emperor,
a message locked inside.

Now this creature flies about
the whole world high and wide,
and when he finds the truest girl,
upon his back she'll ride.
A message from the emperor,
a message locked inside.

1989 © CABAT

No Alligator

You may as well learn this sooner as later:
I'm Ankylosaurus, not an alligator.
I know that I look like a slightly wet pup,
'cause sometimes people will get us mixed up.

I don't snap at swimmers, I'm really quite shy,
no polliwog suppers, I let them swim by.
I like who I am and I might even smile,
if you wouldn't call me a cute crocodile!

Ankylosaurus
ang-KILE-uh-sawr-us

An Old, Old Friend

I'm Sir Edmontonia. I'm really antique;
I lived in an age that was very unique,
with no cars or TVs, just mountains and rocks,
and no schools or bedtime—there weren't any clocks!

We hunted and fished, there was no time to play,
now everything's drastically different today.
If I lived in your time, it sure would be neat;
I'd go to the movies with skates on my feet!

I'd try out for baseball and hit a home run,
or drop in at your house, it sure would be fun.
We'd eat a whole pizza and turn off the lights
and stay up 'til midnight to have pillow fights!

Edmontosaurus
ed-MONT-oh-SAW-rus

The Baby Iguanodon

This happy occasion could bring one to tears;
Iguanodon hatched, after four million years.
His mother is dancing, she hops in the sand,
she thought she had two empty eggs on her hands!

She sat like a mule, just as stubborn as that,
she waited so long, she forgot why she sat.
She waited and waited, the years passed her by,
'til suddenly one day, there came a faint cry.

From inside the egg, just as cute as can be,
a dinosaur hatched and said, "Mother, it's me!"
Now millions of parents have said this before:
A baby is something that's worth waiting for!

Iguanodon
ig-WAN-o-don

A Long, Long, Long Neck

Elasmosaurus, what a sight!
Your party clothes are very bright;
your neck is very strong.

When you eat peanut butter 'n jelly,
does any of it reach your belly?
Does it take very long?

Elasmosaurus
ee-laz-mo-SAW-rus

Left-Over Diplocaulus

Now here's a strange story
we're sure you'll agree,
about the last dinosaur,
down in the sea.

When dinosaurs left,
they forgot him behind.
This brave little guy says,
"I really don't mind;
believe me, it isn't as bad as you think,
'cause who'd really want to be labeled extinct?"

If being a left-over creature's my fate,
I'll paint me all over and I'll celebrate!

Now no one forgets him,
seems he got his wish—
he's making new friends
with the tropical fish!

Diplocaulus
dip-luh-KAWL-us

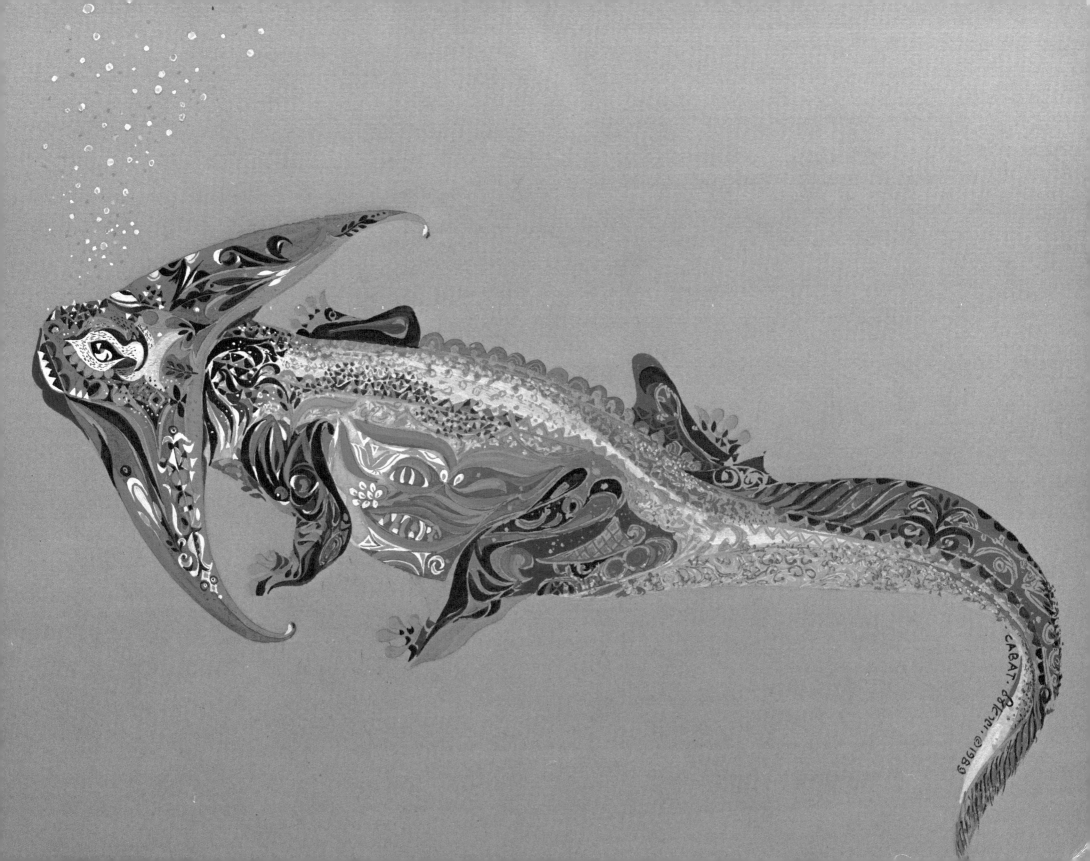

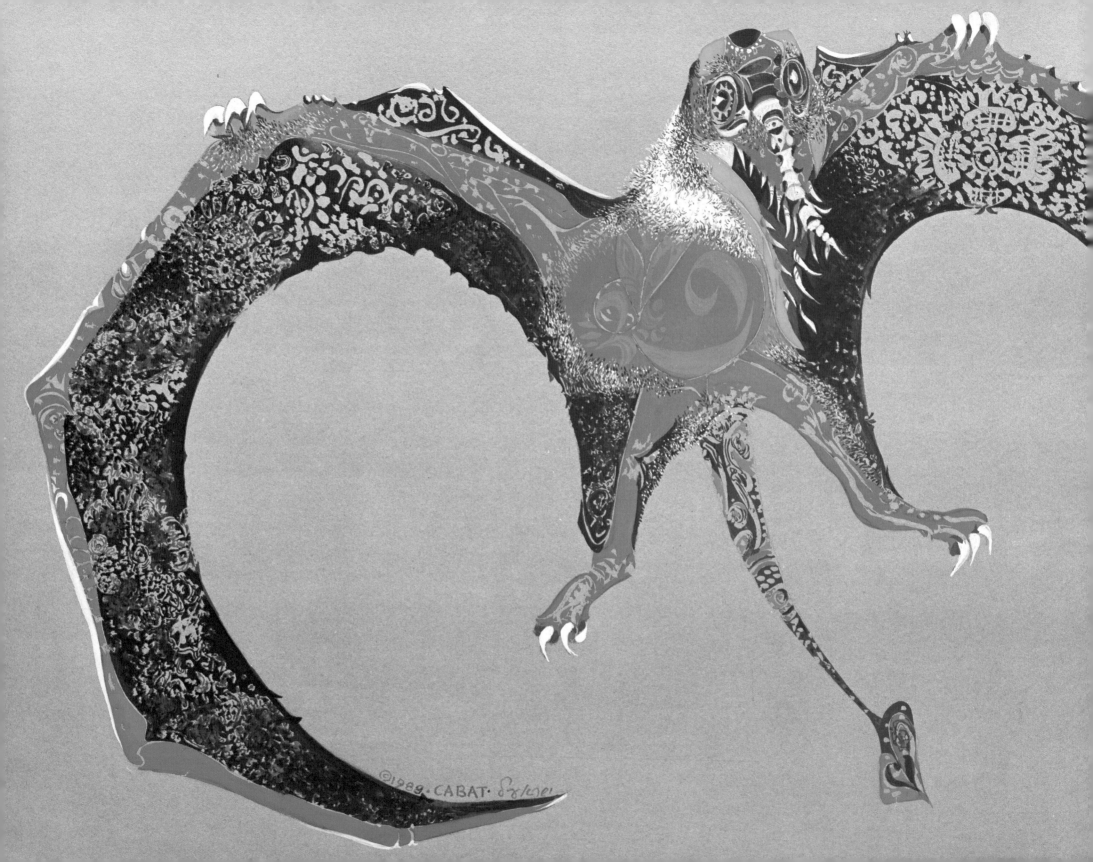

Rhamphorynchus, Ready for the Stage

This fellow looks scary, with wings like a bat.
One day I was walking; he jumped on my hat.
"Which way to New York?" he hissed in my ear.
Now I must confess I was trembling with fear.

"I know there are actors," he said, "on the stage.
I'd make a fine actor and soon be the rage!
I sing and I dance, and I whistle for free.
Not bad for a dinosaur, don't you agree?"

I looked him all over, his head to his toes.
"Take my advice, and you'll get some new clothes,
wax your moustache, curl your hair, trim your nails.
And not many actors on Broadway have tails!"

Before he flew off he said, "Thanks a whole bunch.
Come up to New York soon; we'll have to do lunch!"
It's hard for a struggling young actor today,
but I heard he's a hit in a big Broadway play.

Rhamphorynchus
ram-for-INK-us

Miss Pebbly Beach

Here's Miss Nothosaurus,
she won the first prize,
in a beauty contest.
She's cute for her size!

She swims and she rides
every wave within reach;
now everyone calls her
Miss Pebbly Beach.

Her skin's smooth as gravel,
she never wears clothes,
her perfume's delightful—
it smells like your toes!

It isn't surprising,
now don't you be jealous,
at parties or picnics,
she wins all the fellas.

So line up, you cuties,
and paint your nails peach;
you too could be crowned
Miss Pebbly Beach.

Nothosaurus
no-THO-saw-rus

Bugsy

Hello!

I'm Kuehnosaurus,
I'm quite a nice fellow;
I never throw rocks and
my manners are mellow.

My friends say I'm strange,
though I'm really quite sweet,
since bugs are the things
that I most like to eat.

I eat bugs like popcorn,
and I don't like to boast,
but I eat bugs for breakfast,
with coffee and toast.

Beetles with ice cream,
and roaches with eggs;
spiders that tickle
with eighty-nine legs.

Wiggly-worm sandwiches
and chocolate ant shakes!
I don't care for birds,
and I sure don't like snakes.

When ordering out,
it really takes nerve,
to ask at nice restaurants,
"What bugs do you serve?"

Fleas smeared with mustard
are really a treat;
for brunch I like pickled
grasshopper feet!

So if you start itching
and you have a hunch
there are bugs in your rugs,
invite me to lunch!

Kuehnosaurus
ken-ee-oh-SAW-rus

Speedy Gallimimus

At sixty miles per hour
my feet can really run;
a ride upon my shoulders
for you would sure be fun.

I'm rather strange to look at,
a bill just like a duck;
I have no horn or headlights,
but I'm faster than a truck!

So check your new-car dealers,
in future you may see,
since I'm so sleek and speedy,
a car named after me.

Gallimimus

GAL-ih-MIME-us

© 1989 · CABAT ·

Meganeura, The Insect Queen

High rainbow bridges
and rain on my wings;
traveling through time,
I can fly through these things!
I could climb up over
or under them too:
Red, orange, green, yellow,
bright violet and blue,
my wings look like rainbows
because I fly through.

When dragonflies see me
they stop and they stare;
they call me the old insect
queen of the air.
I'm not only biggest,
the longest, the lightest;
with these neon wings,
I am also the brightest.

When high rainbow bridges
appear in the blue,
look up in the sky
and you might see me too!

Meganeura
meg-uh-NEW-ra

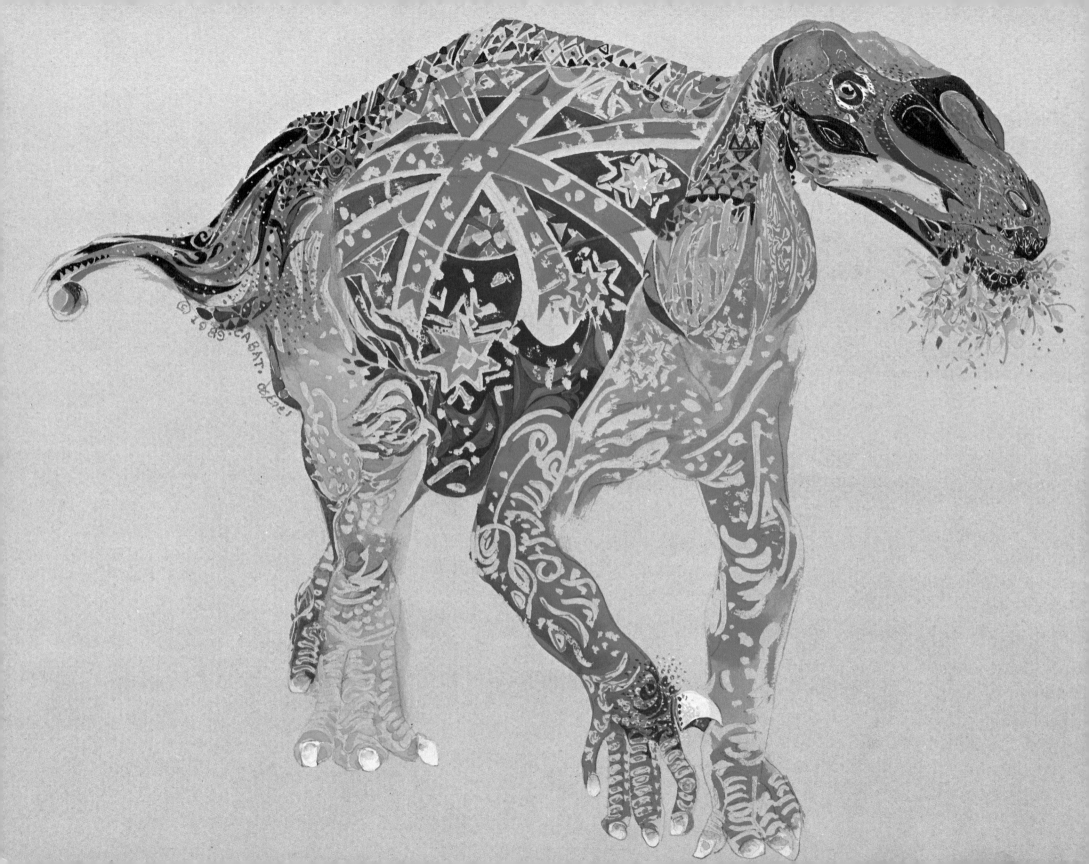

Muttaburrasaurus, The Proud Australian

Australia is where I was born
and just in case you wonder,
it's in the middle of the sea,
the land they call Down Under.

Where every mate's a friend indeed
and kangaroos go hopping,
and everyone buys kiwi fruit
whenever they go shopping.

Australia's in the hemisphere
where skies are blue and fair;
in eucalyptus forests lives
the cute koala bear.

I'm proud to be an Aussie
where kangaroos play tag.
In fact I'm so proud of it
I wear my country's flag!

Muttaburrasaurus
moot-uh-burr-uh-SAW-rus

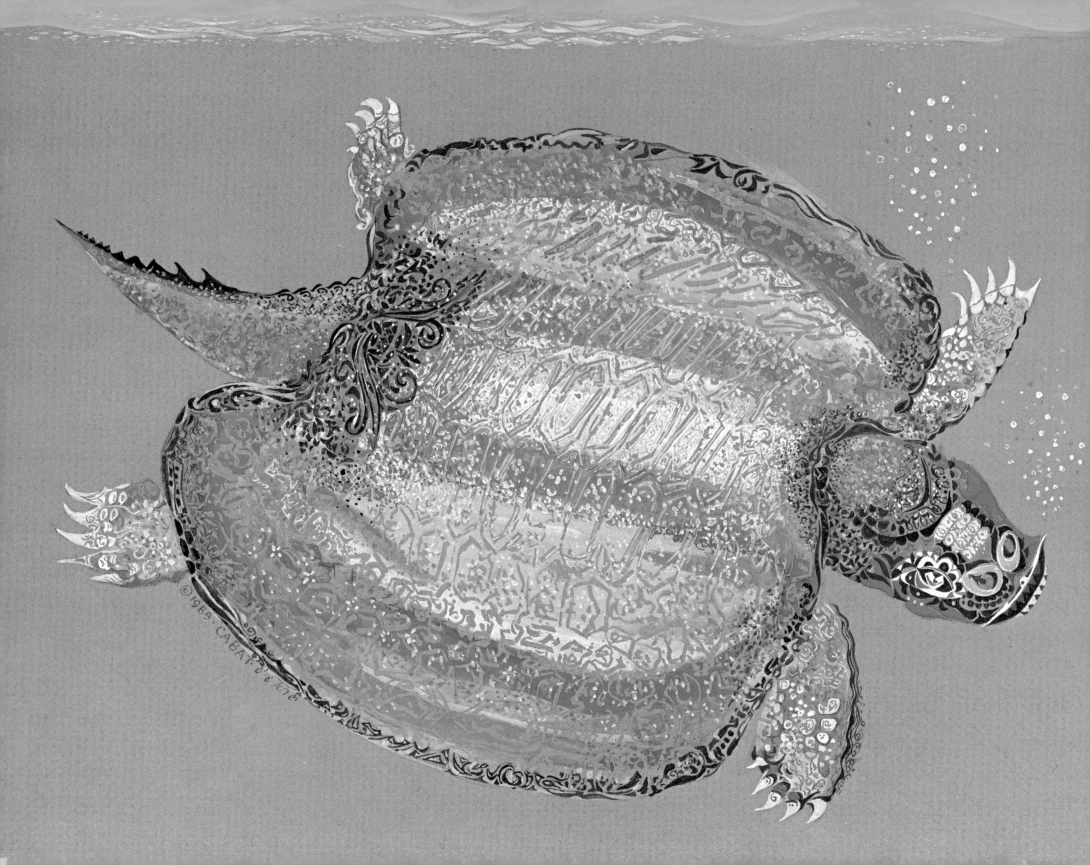

Grandfather Henodus

When planets and stars dreamed of you and of me,
Great-grandfather Henodus lived in the sea.

He swam and he fished and his bubbles went "pop,"
And when he got tired, he'd float to the top.

To visit with friends. (His best friend was a frog;
they'd sit and tell stories on top of a log.)

His ways would seem funny to you and to me,
but he never read papers; there was no TV!

He smoked no cigars and he drank lemon tea,
and he lived to the age of one hundred and three.

Henodus
hen-NO-dus

The Colorful Breath of Anchisaurus

The purple of onions,
bright yellow of cheese.
Won't you brush your teeth,
Mr. Dinosaur, please?

Now don't be offended,
your smile we adore,
but when you say, "Hi, there,"
we faint on the floor!

Red chile spaghetti,
blue garlic by bunch.
(We'll know if we kiss you
what you had for lunch.)

When dinosaurs visit
they travel in haste,
so here, share a tube of
our favorite toothpaste!

Anchisaurus
AN-ki-SAW-rus

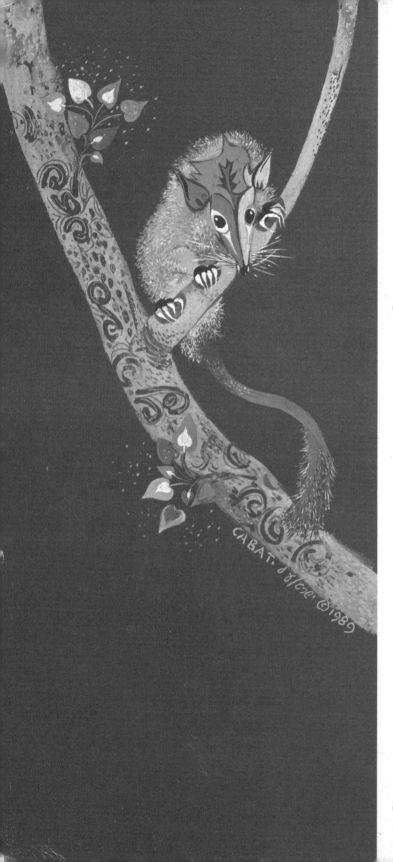

Shrew

The King

I'm King Tyrannosaurus Rex,
and king I'll always be.
A twenty-foot-tall dinosaur,
a fearsome sight to see.

My teeth are eight sharp inches long.
(My nails need trimming too.)
For such a giant dinosaur,
what little arms I grew!

If I came knocking at your door,
your eyes would surely pop,
but my time's gone, and even kings
cannot turn back the clock.

Some ninety million years ago,
I ruled from sea to sea.
Now science has me by the tail,
and time's caught up with me.

So here's my last great royal roar,
from me, I hope you'll learn:
The earth was meant for us to share;
now it's the mammals' turn.

Tyrannosaurus Rex
tie-ran-o-SORE-us REX

GLOSSARY

Anchisaurus
AN-ki-SAW-rus . . . "near reptile"
Late Triassic period, 190 million years ago
6½ feet long
probably an omnivore (meat- and plant-eater)

Ankylosaurus
ang-KILE-uh-sawr-us . . . "stiffened reptile"
Cretaceous period, 65 million years ago
30 feet long, 9 feet high
herbivore (plant-eater)

Archaeopteryx
are-key-OP-ter-ix . . . "ancient wing"
Jurassic period, 150 million years ago
9 feet long, 2 feet high
ate lizards and butterflies

Brachiosaurus
BRACK-ee-oh-SAW-rus . . . "arm reptile"
Jurassic period, 140 million years ago
90 feet long, 40 feet high
herbivore (plant-eater)

Chasmosaurus
KAZ-muh-SAW-rus . . . "opening reptile"
Late Cretaceous period, 70 million years ago
17 feet long
herbivore (plant-eater)

Dimetrodon
dye-MET-tro-don . . . "two long teeth"
Permian period, 260 million years ago
10 feet long, 5 feet high
carnivore (meat-eater)

Diplocaulus
dip-luh-KAWL-us . . . "double shaft"
Late Permian period, 225 million years ago
2 feet long
insectivore (insect-eater)

Edmontosaurus
ed-MONT-oh-SAW-rus . . . "reptile from Edmonton"
Late Cretaceous period, 65-70 million years ago
33-42 feet long
herbivore (plant-eater)

Elasmosaurus
ee-laz-mo-SAW-rus . . . "thin-plate lizard"
Early Jurassic period, 190 million years ago
40 feet long
fish-eater

Gallimimus
GAL-ih-MIME-us . . . "rooster mimic"
Late Cretaceous period, 70 million years ago
13 feet long
omnivore (meat- and plant-eater)

Henodus

hen-NO-dus . . . "single tooth"
Late Triassic period, 190 million years ago
3-4 feet long
ate small crustaceans (shellfish)

Hesperornis

hes-per-OR-nis . . . "western bird"
Late Cretaceous period, 70 million years ago
6 feet long
fish-eater

Iguanodon

ig-WAN-o-don..."lizard tooth"
Cretaceous period, 130 million years ago
25 feet long, 15 feet high
herbivore (plant-eater)

Kuehnosaurus

ken-ee-oh-SAW-rus . . . "Kühne's reptile"
Late Triassic period, 190 million years ago
size unknown
diet unknown

Lambeosaurus

LAM-bee-oh-SAW-rus . . . "Lambe's reptile"
Late Cretaceous period, 70 million years ago
50 feet long
herbivore (plant-eater)

Meganeura

meg-uh-NEW-ra . . . "big-veined"
Late Carboniferous period, 280 million years ago
27½-inch wingspan
insectivore (insect-eater)

Muttaburrasaurus

moot-uh-burr-uh-SAW-rus . . . "Muttaburra
(town in Queensland, Australia) lizard"
Cretaceous period, 70 million years ago
23 feet long, 10 feet high at hip
probably an omnivore (meat- and plant-eater)

Nothosaurus

no-THO-saw-rus . . . "spurious lizard"
Triassic period, 210 million years ago
10 feet long
fish-eater

Oviraptor

o-vee-RAP-tor . . . "egg stealer"
Late Cretaceous period, 70 million years ago
6 feet long
egg-eater

Pachycephalosaurus

PAK-ee-CEF-al-oh-SAW-rus . . . "thick-headed reptile"
Cretaceous period, 75 million years ago
26 feet long
herbivore (plant-eater)

Quetzalcoatlus
ket-sul-co-AT-lus . . . "feathered serpent"
Mesozoic period, 136-225 million years ago
50-foot wingspan
fish-eater

Rhamphorynchus
ram-for-INK-us . . . "narrow beak"
Late Jurassic period, 150 million years ago
18-inch body, 4-foot wingspan
fish-eater

Stegosaurus
STEG-uh-saw-rus . . . "plated reptile"
Early Jurassic to late Cretaceous period,
70-150 million years ago
30 feet long, 16 feet high
herbivore (plant-eater)

Triceratops
try-SER-uh-tops . . . "three-horned face"
Late Cretaceous period, 70 million years ago
30 feet long, 10 feet high. Head was 8 feet long.
herbivore (plant-eater)

Tyrannosaurus Rex
tie-ran-o-SORE-us REX . . . "tyrant reptile"
Late Cretaceous period
60 feet long, 20 feet high
carnivore (meat-eater)

PLEISTOCENE 2 million years ago		**ICE AGE.** Elephants, camels, early man appears.
EOCENE 65 million years ago		Dinosaurs extinct. Mammals become dominant. Horses and primates appear.
CRETACEOUS 135 million years ago		Early mammals, flowering plants appear.
JURASSIC 190 million years ago		Dinosaurs dominate. Flying reptiles and birds appear. Primitive mammals.
TRIASSIC 225 million years ago		Dinosaurs appear. Reptiles dominate.
PERMIAN 280 million years ago		Development of reptiles.
CARBONIFEROUS 350 million years ago		Insects abundant. First reptiles appear. Primitive conifers, lush plant life.
DEVONIAN 395 million years ago		Age of the fish. First amphibians.

Other books from Great Impressions . . .

Erni Cabat's Magical World of Prehistoric Animals.
Twenty-five full-color, full-page paintings of prehistoric
animals by Erni Cabat with whimsical poetry by Lollie Butler.
12″ x 9″, 64 pages, hardcover with dust jacket.
ISBN 0-925263-02-8   **$16.95**

The Flowering Southwest: Wildflowers, Cacti and Succulents in
Arizona, California, Colorado, Nevada, New Mexico, Texas and Utah.
Forty-eight full-color paintings of Southwestern flowering plants.
6″ x 9″, 128 pages, hardcover with dust jacket.
ISBN 0-925263-00-1   **$16.95**

Available from your favorite bookstore or from the publisher.

P.O. Box 65270 / Tucson, Arizona 85740-2270
Telephone (602) 882-5100 / FAX (602) 624-8516